Copyright © 2021 by Lola Muhammad

All rights reserved. No part of this book may be reproduced or used in any manner without written permission of the copyright owner except for the use of quotations in a book review. For more information, address: BOBAcademy@yahoo.com

FIRST EDITION
Print Hardback ISBN 978-1-7369629-3-0
Print Paperback ISBN 978-1-7369629-4-7
eBook ISBN 978-1-7369629-5-4

Instagram: B. O. B. Academy
Facebook: B O B Academy

Black Owned Business Academy

Marketing

Lola Muhammad

There is so much to learn when it comes to the science of business and B.O.B. Academy is here to teach all there is to know.

One way to attract a line of customers to a business is through the use of
MARKETING.

Have you noticed a long line in front of a store before?

WHAT IS MARKETING?

Marketing is a very important business strategy. It is the promotion or advertising of a product or service. A lot of research goes into finding the best marketing strategy for a business. What works for one may not work for another. Because of this, some businesses hire a team to be responsible for their marketing.

MARKET SEGMENTATION

A key factor in marketing is segmentation (seg-min-tay-shun). Market segmentation is dividing possible customers into categories. These categories may include age, gender, interest, and behavior. This helps a business choose the best way to market their product or service to different customers.

What other categories can customers be placed in?

EXAMPLE

For example, a business may market a toy to children by focusing on how fun the toy is to play with. However, a business may market a toy to parents by focusing on how safe the toy is during play.

NICHE MARKETING

This leads into a marketing strategy called niche (neesh) marketing. Niche marketing is when a business focuses on a particular category of people to sell to.

An example is a business selling vegetarian food. The particular category of people they are focusing on are customers who do not eat meat.

ADVERTISEMENTS

There are different ways to market a product or service. One popular way is through advertisements (ad-vur-tyz-mints). Advertisements are avenues of promotion, often public, meant to persuade people's interest in a product or service. This includes TV commercials, posters, and billboards.

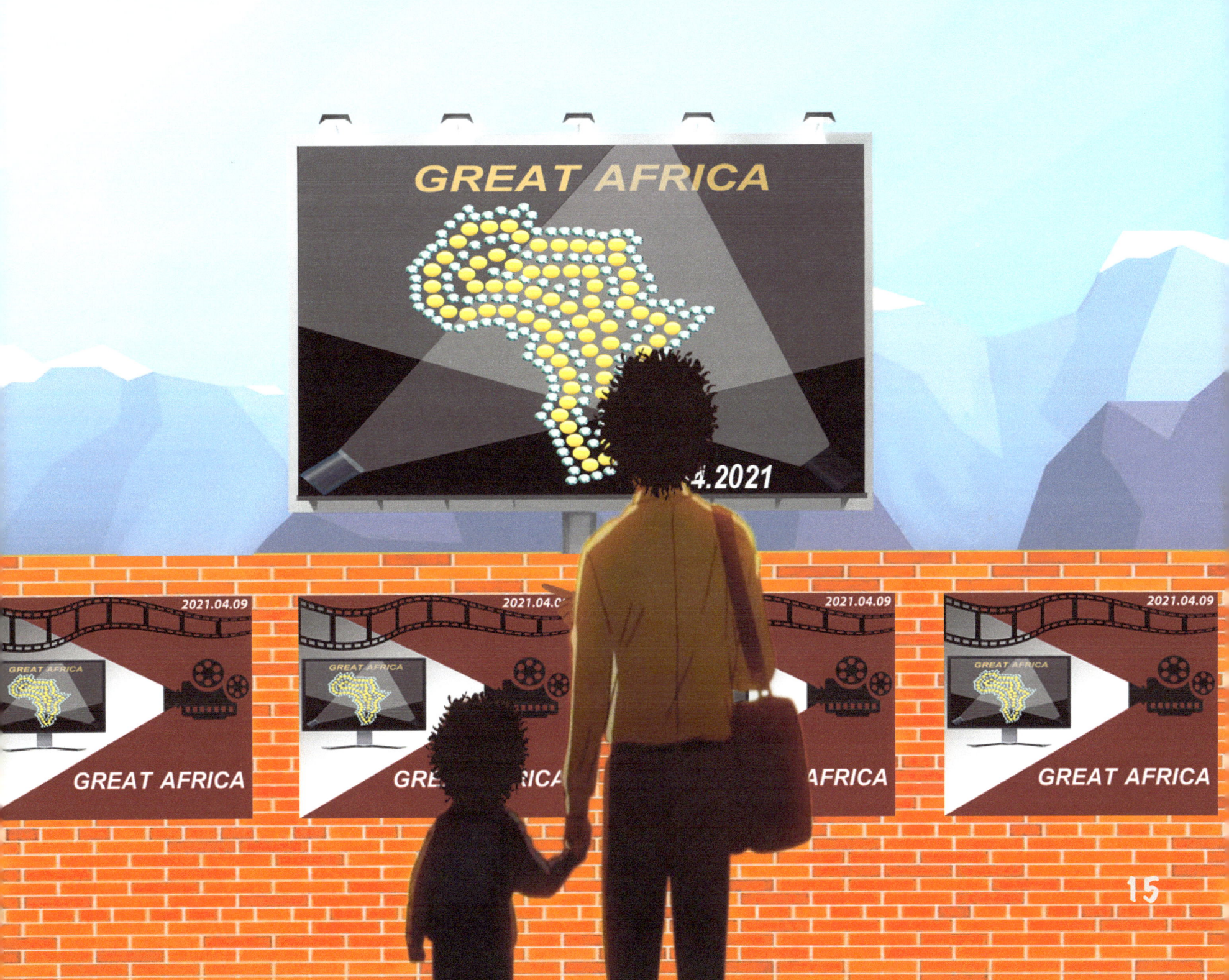

SAMPLES

Another marketing strategy is offering free samples. This is when a business allows possible customers to try their product or service for free. If the customer is satisfied, they may purchase what they have sampled.

SALE

Have you heard of a product or service going on sale? Well, that can also be a marketing strategy. A sale is when a product or service is sold at a discounted price for a limited time.

POSITIVE REVIEWS

Positive reviews can be used for marketing as well. If past customers share their satisfaction with a product or service, others may use their feedback as a reason to trust the business and what the business sells.

I LOVE THIS STORE

REWARD PROGRAMS

Marketing is also used towards customers who have already bought a product or service from a business. Reward programs are a marketing method used in that situation. This motivates customers to return and purchase more products or services. It works by rewarding customers for the purchases they make from the business. This could be done by rewarding customers with points for every purchase. Once a customer gets a certain number of points, a higher reward is earned. This may be a coupon, gift certificate, or free item.

There are many marketing strategies. Businesses may choose more than one if it will help increase customers and sales.

Which marketing strategy catches your attention the most?

FUN FACT

TLC Beatrice International is said to be the first Black-owned billion-dollar company.

ABOUT THE AUTHOR

Lola Muhammad is the author of the Black-owned Business (B.O.B.) Academy series. She has an MBA (Master of Business Administration degree) and completed her MBA Capstone Business Simulation, achieving a ranking in the top ten percentile in the country. She also has certificates in Project Management and Lean Six Sigma, while being a member of the National Black MBA Association (NBMBAA).
Lola has worked with children for over fifteen years and has three children of her own. She understands the importance of business and places value on learning the science of it at an early age.

www.ingramcontent.com/pod-product-compliance
Lightning Source LLC
Chambersburg PA
CBHW041820080526

44589CB00004B/69